100 Things

you should know about

Rainforests

100 Things

you should know about

Rainforests

Camilla de la Bedoyere

Consultant: Barbara Taylor

MASON CREST PUBLISHERS INC.
370 Reed Road
Broomall, Pennsylvania 19008
(866)MCP-BOOK (toll free)
www.masoncrest.com

ISBN: 978-1-4222-2004-7
Series ISBN (15 titles): 978-1-4222-1993-5

First Printing
9 8 7 6 5 4 3 2 1

Cataloging-in-Publication Data on file with the Library of Congress.
Printed in the U.S.A.

First published in 2009 by Miles Kelly Publishing Ltd
Bardfield Centre, Great Bardfield, Essex CM7 4SL

Editorial Director: Belinda Gallagher

Art Director: Jo Brewer

Managing Editor: Rosie McGuire

Editorial Assistant: Claire Philip

Volume Designer: Sophie Pelham

Image Manager: Lorraine King

Indexer: Jane Parker

Production Manager: Elizabeth Brunwin

Reprographics: Ian Paulyn

ACKNOWLEDGEMENTS
The publishers would like to thank the following artists
who have contributed to this book:
Ian Jackson, Mike Foster
All other artwork from the Miles Kelly Artwork Bank

The publishers would like to thank the following
sources for the use of their photographs:

Cover Fritz Polking/FLPA; Page 6 Siegfried Layda/Getty Images; 8–9 Nigel J Dennis/NHPA;
10 (l) Owen Franken/Corbis, (r) urosr/Fotolia; 11 (main) Frans Lanting/Corbis, (tr) Demetrio Carrasco/JAI/Corbis;
12–13 Nick Gibson/Photolibrary; 12 (bl inset) amaet/Fotolia; 13(r inset) Impala/Fotolia;
18–19 (t) Wave RF/Photolibrary; 19 (tr) Mark Moffett/Minden Pictures/FLPA, (br) Sergio Pitamitz/Photolibrary;
21 Paul Raffaele/Rex Features; 22–23 (t) Roy Toft/Getty Images; 24 (t) Sloth92/Dreamstime, (b) fivespots/Fotolia;
25 (tr) Martin Harvey/Corbis, (b) Frans Lanting/FLPA; 26 (bl) Jeffrey Oonk/Minden Pictures/FLPA;
29 (tr) Mike Powles/Photolibrary; 30 (l) David M Dennis/Photolibrary, (r) Garcia Garcia/Photolibrary;
31 (br) David Kirkland/Photolibrary; 32–33 Wendy Shattil/Photolibrary; 34–35 J & C Sohns/Photolibrary;
34 (bl) Morales Morales/Photolibrary; 36 (tc) Michael Luckett/Fotolia; 40–41 ImageBroker/Imagebroker/FLPA;
41(tl) Shariff Che'Lah/Fotolia, (tc) Braendan/Dreamstime, (tr) Uros Petrovic/Fotolia, (br) George Steinmetz/Corbis;
42–43 Cyril Ruoso/JH Editorial/Minden Pictures/FLPA; 43 (tr) NHPA/Martin Harvey; 44 Frans Lanting/Corbis;
45 (main) Jacques Jangoux/Photolibrary; 46 (tr) Matthias Clamer/Getty Images, (b) BrazilPhotos.com/Alamy;
47 Berndt Fischer/Photolibrary

All other photographs are from:

Corel, digitalSTOCK, digitalvision, iStockphoto.com, John Foxx, PhotoAlto,
PhotoDisc, PhotoEssentials, PhotoPro, Stockbyte

Contents

1 In the world's rainforests animals and plants are closely linked in a daily struggle for survival. It's a battle for life that has been going on for millions of years, and has led to these unique environments becoming home to a huge variety of living things, from the deadliest frogs to the foulest-smelling flowers.

▼ In a rainforest, plants of all types fight for light and space. They create an emerald-green landscape of leafy undergrowth and towering trees.

What is a rainforest?

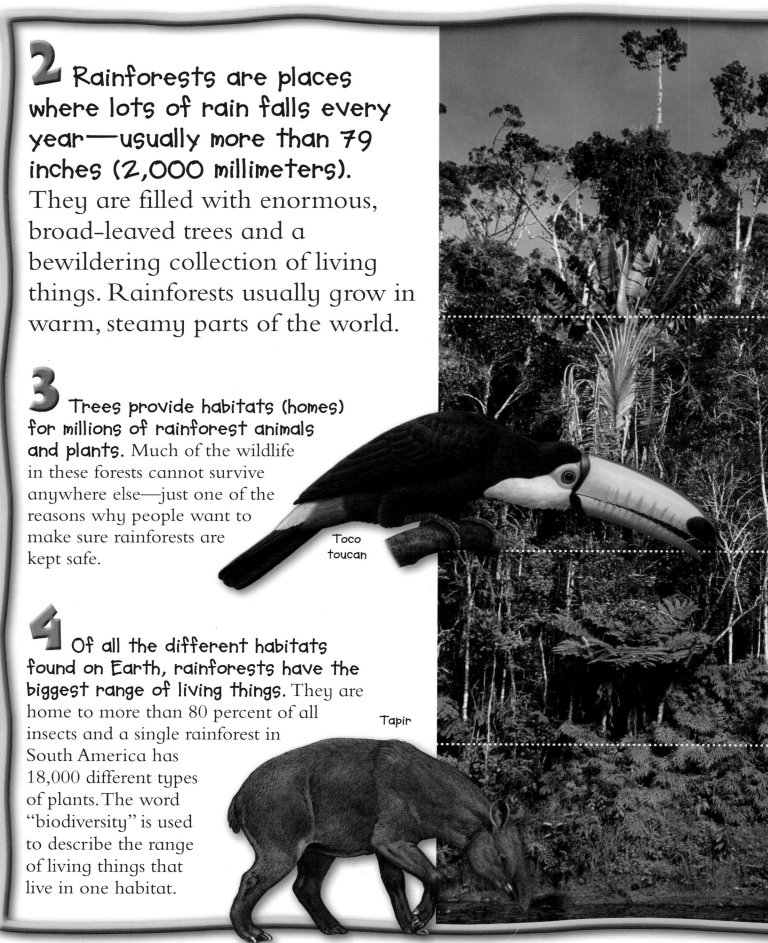

2 Rainforests are places where lots of rain falls every year—usually more than 79 inches (2,000 millimeters). They are filled with enormous, broad-leaved trees and a bewildering collection of living things. Rainforests usually grow in warm, steamy parts of the world.

3 Trees provide habitats (homes) for millions of rainforest animals and plants. Much of the wildlife in these forests cannot survive anywhere else—just one of the reasons why people want to make sure rainforests are kept safe.

Toco toucan

4 Of all the different habitats found on Earth, rainforests have the biggest range of living things. They are home to more than 80 percent of all insects and a single rainforest in South America has 18,000 different types of plants. The word "biodiversity" is used to describe the range of living things that live in one habitat.

Tapir

Queen Alexandra's
birdwing butterfly

5 Rainforests have four main layers. The bottom layers are the dark, dank forest floor and understory, where the shortest plants live. Here, bugs, frogs, fungi and many other living things thrive. The middle layer is the forest canopy and the top layer is the emergent layer. This is where the tallest trees poke up above a blanket of green leaves. The trees are home to vines, mosses, monkeys, lizards, snakes, insects and thousands of species (types) of bird.

◀ Most animals and plants live in the rainforest canopy layer. The understory is very gloomy because not much sunlight reaches it.

I DON'T BELIEVE IT!

People who live in rainforests can build their entire homes from plant materials. Walls are made from palm stems or bamboo and leaves can be woven to make roofs and floors.

Red-eyed tree frog

6 Rainforests are home to people as well as animals and plants. Many tribes (groups of people) live in these dense, green forests around the world, finding food, medicines and shelter among the trees. Some of them still follow a traditional lifestyle, hunting animals and gathering plants for food.

7 Hot, steamy rainforests are sometimes called jungles. They are found in Earth's tropical regions. These are areas near the Equator, an imaginary line that encircles the Earth, where daily temperatures are around 77° F (25° C) and it rains most days.

▼ A boy rows a canoe made from a hollow tree trunk on the Amazon River in Brazil.

8 Around 60–100 million years ago, most of the world's land was covered with tropical rainforest. Now only a tiny area—six percent—is covered. This is partly due to deforestation (people cutting down trees) and partly because the Earth's climate has changed, becoming cooler and drier.

9 Temperate rainforests grow in cool, wet places. "Temperate" means having a moderate climate. Trees here are usually conifers such as pine trees. Temperate rainforests are home to the world's largest trees—Californian redwoods. These can live for 2,000 years, and the tallest reach 377 feet (115 meters) in height.

▶ Redwoods, or sequoias, are giant trees that sprout from tiny seeds. The trees produce cones that each contain up to 300 seeds.

► Mangrove trees grow long and tangled roots, which slow down the movement of water and create a habitat for animals.

10 **Mangrove swamps are another type of warm, wet rainforest.** The trees that grow here live with their roots steeped in layers of mud, silt and salty water. Around half of the world's mangrove forests have been cut down in the last 50 years and it is expected that almost all mangrove forests will have disappeared by 2050.

11 **Rainforests on mountains higher than 8,200 feet (2,500 meters) are often shrouded in mist.** They are given the name "cloud forests," and here the temperatures are lower than in a tropical rainforest. Mosses, ferns and liverworts are plants that thrive in these permanently damp conditions. The trunk and branches of a tree in a cloud forest can be completely covered in a bright-green coating of moss.

► Cloud forests can be eerie places where trees and plants are permanently shrouded in a fine mist.

HUG A TREE!

Visit a local woodland or forest and find out the names of some of its trees. Use a sketchbook or camera to record images of wildlife you see there. Find out which are the widest tree trunks by hugging them. Can you find one that is so broad your fingers don't touch?

Where in the world?

12 Tropical forests grow in the region close to the Equator. The area just south of the Equator is called the Tropic of Capricorn, and the area just north of the Equator is called the Tropic of Cancer.

NORTH AMERICA

▼ Grizzly bears live in forests near the Pacific coast and hunt salmon in the cold, fresh rivers.

Equator

SOUTH AMERICA

13 Wet winds and cool fogs from the Pacific Ocean sweep onto the coast of North America, creating the perfect climate for temperate rainforests. This is ideal for giant conifers—evergreen trees that live there. The forests are home to black bears, mountain lions and blacktail deer.

14 Amazonia is the huge tropical rainforest of Brazil and neighboring South American countries. Further south, temperate rainforests grow, cloaked in cold mist. In the Chilean temperate rainforests, ancient trees called alerces grow. The oldest alerce is thought to have lived for over 4,000 years.

◀ Piranhas are sharp-toothed Amazon fish. They feed on a variety of animals including other fish and snails.

◀ Atlas moths are the world's largest moths. They flutter through the canopies of Asian cloud forests.

EUROPE

ASIA

▼ Cassowaries are large birds that cannot fly. They live in the forests of Australia and New Guinea.

AFRICA

◀ African bush vipers live in the forest canopy, slithering down to hunt frogs and lizards.

OCEANIA

15 Cloud forests usually grow on, or near, mountain ranges, where there is plenty of rain and mist. In China, the Yunnan cloud forest grows over tall mountains and deep gorges. The name *Yunnan* means "south of the clouds"—it's a mysterious place that few people have visited.

QUIZ

1. What is the Equator?
2. Where does the cassowary live?
3. How old is the oldest-known alerce?

KEY   Tropical forest   Cloud forest   Temperate forest

Tree of life

16 **The brazil–nut tree produces balls of seeds.** Each ball is the size of a melon and as hard as stone. This amazing tree grows in tropical rainforests and provides a home and food for many living things.

17 **When the seed balls are ripe they crash to the ground.** Only the agouti, a dog-sized rodent, has teeth tough enough to break through the case to reach the tasty brazil nuts inside. Agoutis bury some of the nuts, which may then grow into trees. Without agoutis new brazil-nut trees could not grow.

▲ Between 12 and 24 nuts grow inside each brazil–nut tree seed case. Inside each nut is a seed.

Strangler fig

18 **Strangler figs grow up and around the trunks of rainforest trees.** Over years, the fig continues to grow until it eventually strangles its host tree to death. Once the tree has rotted, only the tangled web of fig roots and stems remain, like a spooky tree skeleton.

◄ Agoutis' teeth continue to grow throughout their lives, allowing them to bite through nutshells.

▼ Brazil-nut tree flowers open before sunrise. By the end of the day, all the petals will have fallen off.

20 Brazil-nut trees also depend on a single type of insect to survive—orchid bees. These are the only insects strong enough to get inside the tree's heavy, hooded flowers to pollinate them, so the nuts—which contain seeds—can grow into new plants.

► Female orchid bees visit brazil-nut flowers to feed on nectar, while male orchid bees visit orchids to collect perfume.

19 Fallen leaves at the base of tropical trees quickly disappear. Dead matter, called leaf litter, is broken down by fungi, or eaten by bugs. This process is known as decomposition, and it helps the goodness from the leaves return to the forest soil in a natural method of recycling.

Male orchid bee

21 When a number of different living things all depend on one another for survival they are described as an ecosystem. Rainforest habitats are large ecosystems, and a brazil-nut tree is a small ecosystem. When brazil-nut trees are cut down, many other living things that depend on them die, too.

◄ A brazil-nut tree can grow to 200 feet (60 meters) in height and produce more than 220 pounds (100 kilograms) of nuts every year.

Amazing Amazon

22 **The Amazon rainforest is the largest tropical rainforest in the world.** It covers 2.3 million square miles (6 million square kilometers), which means it is nearly the same size as Australia. Around half of all animal and plant species live in Amazonia, as this forest is known.

23 **The giant Amazon River wends its way through the forest, bringing life and death to many of its inhabitants.** This is the world's biggest river, stretching for about 4,000 miles (6,400 kilometers) and pouring 203 billion gallons (770 billion liters) of water into the Atlantic Ocean every day. People and animals of the forest use the river for transport, food and water.

◄ An Amazonian Hercules beetle can grow to 7 inches (18 centimeters) in length. It is one of the world's largest insects.

24 **Insect experts who traveled to Amazonia in the 1840s discovered more than 8,000 new species (types) of beetle.** Alfred Wallace and Henry Bates were among the first of many scientists who realized that this rainforest has a fantastic range of animal and plant life, many of which do not exist anywhere else. Charles Darwin, a 19th century scientist, described it as "a great wild, untidy, luxuriant hothouse."

▼ The Amazon River basin holds 20 percent of the world's fresh water.

25 **The waters of the Amazon are home to many types of animal and plant.** Giant waterlilies with 6.6-foot-wide (2-meter-wide) leaves grow in slow-moving stretches of the river, but just beneath them lurk hungry alligators, sharp-toothed piranha fish and blood-sucking leeches.

26 **There are more than 400 species of reptile, such as snakes and lizards, in the Amazon rainforest.** More freshwater fish live in the Amazon River than anywhere else on Earth, and more than 225 types of amphibian, such as frogs and toads, live in and around the water.

► Large green iguanas like to lie on branches that hang over the Amazon River and soak up the sun's warming rays.

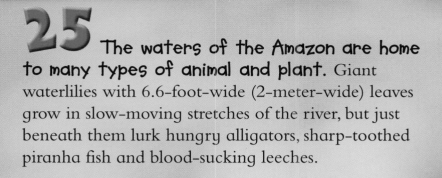

I DON'T BELIEVE IT!
Giant Amazonian leeches are blood-sucking worms that can grow up to 12 inches (30 centimeters) in length! They have sharp teeth and pain-numbing spit that stops blood from clotting so they can enjoy a long feast.

People of the Amazon

27 The Amazon was given its name by a Spanish explorer who ventured down the river in the 1540s. Francisco de Orellana was attacked by the local long-haired people who reminded him of the mythical female warriors described by the ancient Greeks, so he named the Amazon after them.

▶ Inside the *shabono*, Yanomani people build circular huts called *malocas*. At night, the young people sleep in hammocks, outside the *malacos*.

28 When Europeans first went to the Amazon rainforest in search of treasure, there were around seven million people living there. Today, 500 years later, there are fewer than a million. The Amazonian people live as groups, or tribes, and have different cultures and languages from one another.

29 The Yanomani people still follow many of their ancient traditions today. Villagers share one large home, known as the *shabono*, and women grow crops such as sweet potatoes. Men hunt using blowpipes and bows and arrows. The rainforest is the children's school, where they learn how to survive in, and protect, their jungle home.

◀ Several families make up one Yanomani village. They live, work and play together, passing on traditions and skills.

30 **The Embera people use the poison produced by rainforest frogs to hunt animals to eat.** Men wipe the tips of their blowpipe darts on the frogs' backs before firing them. One golden poison dart frog has enough poison to kill ten men. In recent years several rainforest frogs have become extinct (died out), but no one knows why this is.

▲ The golden poison frog produces poison on its skin, which the people of the Embera tribe carefully wipe on their darts.

31 **Although many Amazonian people live in protected areas of rainforest, many more face an uncertain future.** Large parts of Amazonia are being taken over by mining and logging companies. They cut down large parts of the forest, forcing local people to move elsewhere.

▶ Embera women clean and prepare food in rivers and lakes, but many have become polluted.

Forests of Oceania

32 Hundreds of millions of years ago there was a giant continent called Gondwana. Around 140 million years ago, Gondwana began to split, and eventually Australia, New Zealand and New Guinea broke away from the rest of the landmass. Wildlife that evolved in these places is very different from that found elsewhere.

33 Walking through the cloud forests of New Guinea is an incredible experience. The air is damp, and every surface is covered with plants, especially mosses and ferns. When the clouds open, torrential rain drenches each living thing.

34 Dragons live in Australia's rainforest, waiting to pounce on passers-by. These are not real dragons, but lizards called Boyd's forest dragons—and they attack bugs, not people! They live on trees, where their patterned scales help them to stay hidden from view.

▶ Australian tree kangaroos scamper through branches. When they are scared, they can jump down from trees in one giant leap.

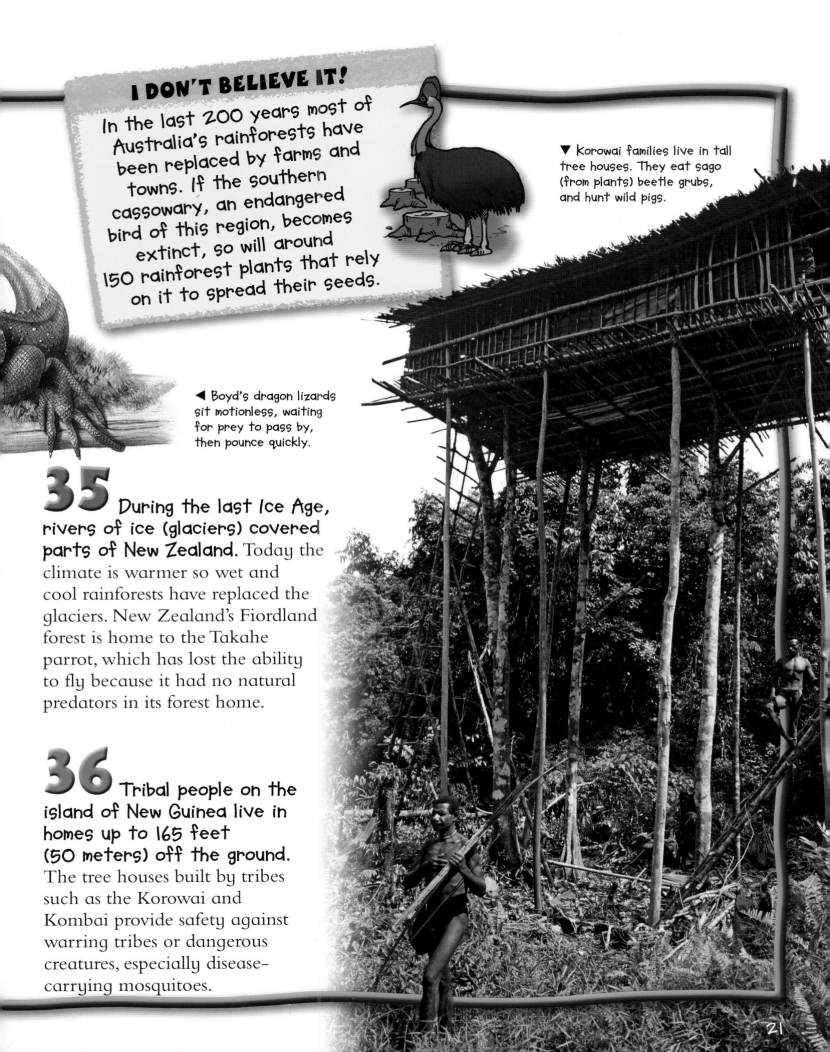

In the last 200 years most of Australia's rainforests have been replaced by farms and towns. If the southern cassowary, an endangered bird of this region, becomes extinct, so will around 150 rainforest plants that rely on it to spread their seeds.

▼ Korowai families live in tall tree houses. They eat sago (from plants) beetle grubs, and hunt wild pigs.

◀ Boyd's dragon lizards sit motionless, waiting for prey to pass by, then pounce quickly.

35 During the last Ice Age, rivers of ice (glaciers) covered parts of New Zealand. Today the climate is warmer so wet and cool rainforests have replaced the glaciers. New Zealand's Fiordland forest is home to the Takahe parrot, which has lost the ability to fly because it had no natural predators in its forest home.

36 Tribal people on the island of New Guinea live in homes up to 165 feet (50 meters) off the ground. The tree houses built by tribes such as the Korowai and Kombai provide safety against warring tribes or dangerous creatures, especially disease-carrying mosquitoes.

Magical Madagascar

37 Madagascar is the world's fourth largest island. It lies to the east of Africa, in the warm waters of the Indian Ocean. The rainforests here cover almost 4,000 square miles (10,000 square kilometers), and are mostly found on the island's eastern coast.

38 When Madagascar split away from the rest of Africa about 165 million years ago, its animals and plants began moving on a unique path of change. Now this tropical place is a haven for some amazing animals such as lemurs and colored lizards called chameleons. Between 80 and 90 percent of the 250,000 species found here live nowhere else, and new species are discovered all the time.

▼ Ring-tailed lemurs live together in groups that are ruled by females. They feed on plants and, unlike most lemurs, spend much of their time on the ground.

39 Lemurs are animals with long legs and bushy tails that leap through trees. They are related to monkeys and apes and, like their cousins, are intelligent and inquisitive creatures. The ring-tailed lemur lives in groups of up to 25 family members. They like to sit in the sun, but scatter if a member of the group sounds an alarm call to warn of danger nearby.

◀ The wings of the African sunset moth are ablaze with beautiful colors. Like most colorful moths, it is active during the day.

40 People have been living on Madagascar for around 2,000 years. Travelers from Arabia, Asia, Africa and Indonesia have all settled here, along with Europeans. Four out of every five adults earns a living from agriculture. More than 90 percent of Madagascar's rainforests have been destroyed to provide farmland for the growing population.

◀ The rosy periwinkle is used to make drugs that fight deadly diseases.

41 The pretty rosy periwinkle plant is found in Madagascar's rainforests and is used to fight cancer. It contains chemicals that are used to make drugs that combat this deadly disease. The rosy periwinkle is endangered in the wild because its forest home has been largely destroyed.

I DON'T BELIEVE IT!

Lemurs in Madagascar have been seen rolling giant millipedes over their fur. No one knew why, until scientists discovered that the many-legged bugs release chemicals that keep flies and fleas off the lemurs—like a natural fly spray!

▶ A Madagascan aye-aye taps a tree with its long middle finger. It listens for sounds of moving grubs beneath, and hooks them out.

42 The Congo rainforest (or Central African rainforest) lies in the center of Africa, in the basin of the Congo River. It is the second largest rainforest, with an area around twice the size of France. More than 50 million people depend on it for survival.

▲ The Central African rainforest is home to more than 11,000 types of plant and 400 types of mammal, such as African forest elephants.

43 Before European explorers ventured into Africa's jungles the native people lived in harmony with their environment. They survived as hunter-gatherers—they only killed what they needed to eat, and collected fruits by hand. Europeans wanted to use the rainforests to make money—a practice that continues today.

44 Walking through the African rainforest is a challenging, frightening, noisy activity! Plants block every step and strange noises come from all corners, including squeaks, trilling, singing, cheeps, growls and roars. Deadly snakes and spiders lurk in dark corners, and biting or stinging insects will sniff out human flesh in seconds.

◀ Gray parrots are common in Arican rainforests, where they feed on fruits and seeds.

45
The Batwa people of Central Africa are pygmies, which means they are unusually short. They have lived in African rainforests for thousands of years, collecting honey and hunting. When farmers destroyed the Batwas' forests, they were left without homes and with no way to get food. Most now live in great poverty.

▶ Some Batwa men still climb trees to collect honey, but most members of the tribe have been forced to leave their forest homes.

46
African hardwoods are prized for their great beauty and durability. These woods come from tropical trees and have been used for centuries to make fine furniture and decorative objects. Mahogany, ebony and teak are all exotic woods from African rainforests.

▼ Around 90 percent of the rainforests in West Africa have been wiped out by farming.

QUIZ

Three of these countries are in Africa, and three are in South America. Can you put them in the right continents?

Colombia Gabon Congo
Guyana Brazil Ghana

Answers:
Africa: Congo Gabon Ghana
South America: Brazil Colombia
Guyana

Forests of the Far East

47 The word "jungle" comes from a Hindi word meaning "thick forest." Most Asian rainforests lie on the mainland, from India to Bhutan and Malaysia, or on tropical islands such as Sumatra.

▼Orangutans live in trees, but they do spend some time on land. They can walk through water, but do not swim.

48 Borneo cloud forests provide shelter and food for one of the world's most endangered apes. Orangutans live in trees and feed on the fruit of more than 400 different types of tree, especially durians and figs. If they can't find fruit, they eat leaves and bark.

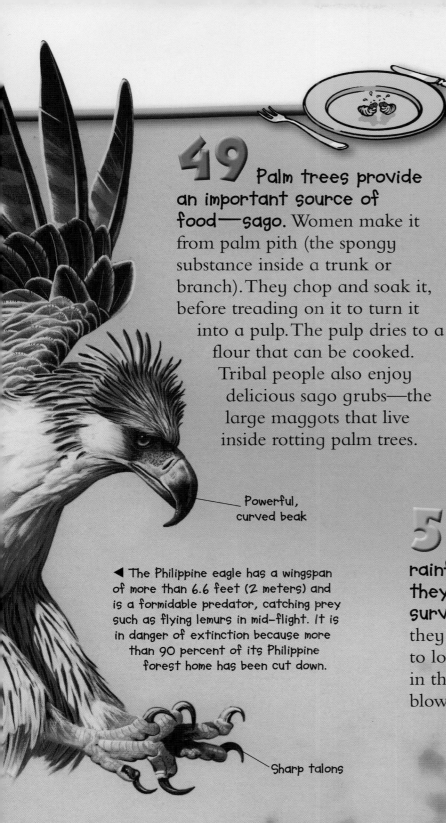

49 Palm trees provide an important source of food—sago. Women make it from palm pith (the spongy substance inside a trunk or branch). They chop and soak it, before treading on it to turn it into a pulp. The pulp dries to a flour that can be cooked. Tribal people also enjoy delicious sago grubs—the large maggots that live inside rotting palm trees.

Powerful, curved beak

◄ The Philippine eagle has a wingspan of more than 6.6 feet (2 meters) and is a formidable predator, catching prey such as flying lemurs in mid-flight. It is in danger of extinction because more than 90 percent of its Philippine forest home has been cut down.

Sharp talons

RAIN RECORD

It rains almost every day in a rainforest. To measure your rainfall you need a clear plastic container, a ruler and a notebook.
1. Place the empty container outside, away from trees.
2. At the same time every day measure the water in the container.
3. Empty your container after each measurement.
4. Record your results in a notebook.

50 The people of the Indonesian rainforests are called Orang Asli and they have had a hard battle for survival in recent times. In Malaysia, they were often captured and sold as slaves to local chiefs. Many Orang Asli still live in the rainforests, hunting monkeys with blowpipes made from bamboo.

Flying lemur

51 Known as the lord of the jungle, the Philippine eagle soars over Asian rainforests, hunting monkeys and squirrels. It is one of the world's biggest raptors (birds of prey), but also one of the most endangered. There are now probably no more than 500 alive.

Cloud forests

52 **Trekking through the Monteverde cloud forest of Costa Rica can be done on foot—or by air!** Visitors can fly between the trees on zip wires, passing through low-lying clouds to get a bird's-eye view of the treetops. On the ground, every surface is wet, as it is either drizzling or pouring with rain for much of the day.

▲ Three-toed sloths are slow-moving mammals. Their camouflage is their only defense against jaguars—the big cats of South America that hunt them.

▼ Mountain gorillas live in the cloud forests of Africa's Virunga National Park. They are highly endangered animals, despite being our close cousins.

53 **At night, cloud forests buzz with life, but the sleepy sloth rarely stirs.** These animals from Central and South America are such slow movers that plants grow in their fur, giving perfect camouflage! Three-toed sloths hang from branches and sleep upside-down for up to 18 hours every day, only coming down to the ground once a week. It takes them one minute to travel just 10 feet (3 meters).

54 Epiphytes are rainforest plants that grow very well in cloud forests. They emerge from the nooks and crannies of tree trunks and branches, to reach more sunlight than they would on the forest floor. Dirt collects in these places and turns to soil. The epiphytes' roots grow into this soil, where they collect nutrients and water.

▲ Trees in cloud forests are covered in epiphytes and they grow roots from their trunks and branches. These hanging roots can be tens of feet in length and absorb water from the damp atmosphere.

◄ In the mating season a male quetzal grows two tail feathers that may reach 3.3 feet (1 meter) in length.

GO SLOW

Measure out 10 feet (3 meters) on the floor. How quickly can you cover this distance when you run? Probably very quickly! Now try to cover the same distance as slowly as you can, so it takes a whole minute—just like a three-toed sloth. Now do it again, upside down (only joking!)

55 As a resplendent quetzal flies through Mexico's cloud forest its tail feathers shimmer in the sunlight. Male quetzals, known as birds of the gods, have the longest tail feathers of any bird in the region, and they are often regarded as one of the world's most beautiful birds. Quetzals eat wild avocados, swallowing the fruit whole. The seeds pass through their bodies, helping new avocado trees to grow.

Peculiar plants

56 It is thought that more than 60 percent of plant species live in rainforests. Plants do an important job in making the soil stable so rain doesn't wash it away. They also take carbon dioxide out of the air, and put oxygen—the gas we breathe—back into it.

◀ Titan arums only grow wild in the Indonesian island of Sumatra. They smell of rotting meat.

▶ Durians are called "kings of fruits" and are eaten in Indonesia and Malaysia.

57 One of the stinkiest plants is the giant titan arum. This freaky flower can grow to 10 feet (3 meters) in height and produces a pungent perfume to attract insects. The insects pollinate the plants so that it can produce seeds. The titan arum only flowers once every seven years.

58 The smell of a ripe durian fruit can be detected nearly one kilometer away. Visitors to the rainforests of Southeast Asia say durians stink like rotting fish, but the local people and the animals don't mind—they know the soft flesh tastes sweet. Tigers, sun bears and mouse deer all eat durians that have fallen to the forest floor.

▶ Look inside a pitcher plant and you can see how it traps bugs.

Slippery surface

59 **Pitcher plants are killers.** These pretty green plants lure bugs using a tempting scent. As insects land on the rim of the pitcher, their feet lose their grip on the waxy surface, sending them tumbling into the trap. The plant produces acid, which digests the insect's body, dissolving it within hours. The enormous rajah pitcher plant can even digest mice and birds!

Insects caught in thick liquid

I DON'T BELIEVE IT!

Scientists recently discovered that the water in a pitcher plant is thickened with slime, which sucks the insect down like quicksand. It may be possible to use this slime to develop chemicals that kill insect pests.

▼ Rafflesia plants are parasites so they do not need roots, stems or leaves. Their foul smell attracts flies that pollinate the flowers.

60 **The biggest flower on Earth—the rafflesia—grows in the rainforests of Borneo.** This monster bloom can reach one meter across and smells of rotting flesh. The rafflesia lives on other plants and steals its food and water from its "host."

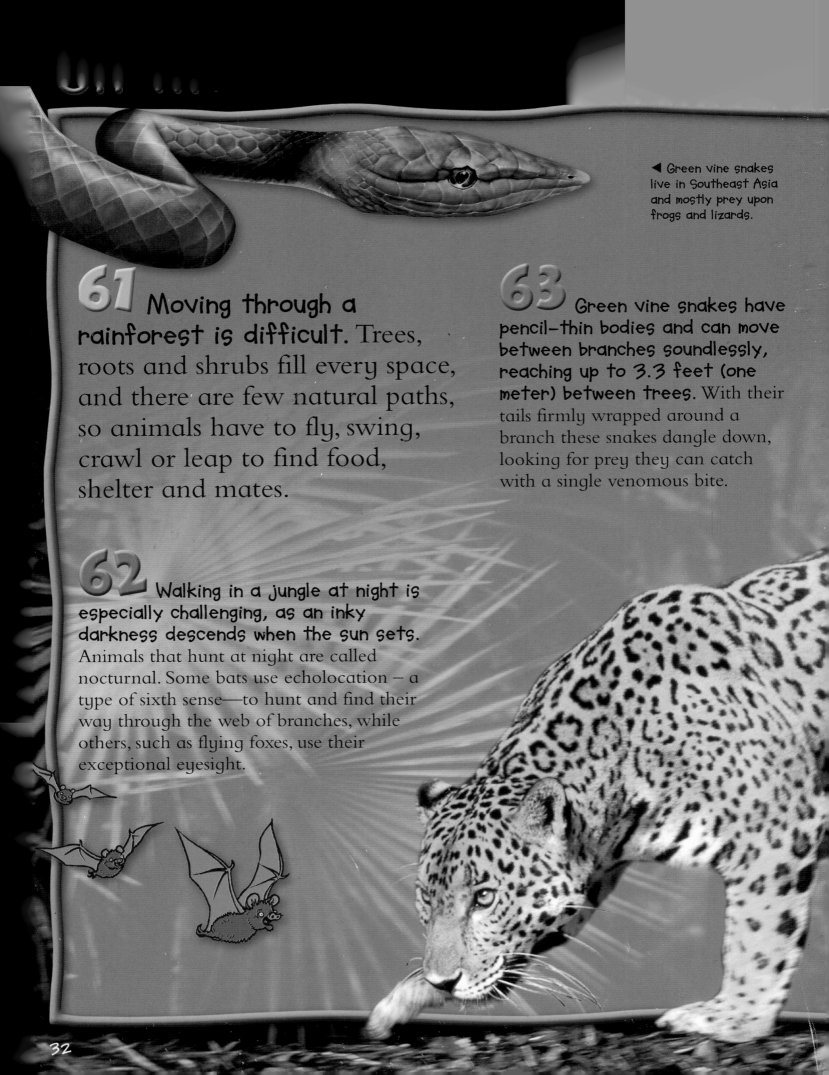

◀ Green vine snakes live in Southeast Asia and mostly prey upon frogs and lizards.

61 Moving through a rainforest is difficult. Trees, roots and shrubs fill every space, and there are few natural paths, so animals have to fly, swing, crawl or leap to find food, shelter and mates.

62 Walking in a jungle at night is especially challenging, as an inky darkness descends when the sun sets. Animals that hunt at night are called nocturnal. Some bats use echolocation – a type of sixth sense—to hunt and find their way through the web of branches, while others, such as flying foxes, use their exceptional eyesight.

63 Green vine snakes have pencil–thin bodies and can move between branches soundlessly, reaching up to 3.3 feet (one meter) between trees. With their tails firmly wrapped around a branch these snakes dangle down, looking for prey they can catch with a single venomous bite.

▲ Gibbons can swing from tree to tree using their long, strong arms. This movement is called brachiation.

64 Geckos can run along branches upside down, thanks to millions of tiny hairs on the soles of their feet. Each hair may be too small to see with the naked eye, but together they create a sticky force that holds the lizard to the tree. Scientists have been able to copy geckos' feet to make a super-sticky tape for use by humans.

65 Monkeys have prehensile (gripping) tails to help them keep their balance on branches. White-faced capuchins are small monkeys that live in groups, scampering through forests looking for bugs and fruit to eat. They can leap from tree to tree, but will sometimes run along the ground while keeping a watchful eye for jaguars.

◄ Like other big cats, jaguars move with stealth and in silence. Fur on their large padded paws helps to dampen the sound of their footsteps.

Quiz

A monkey leaps through the treetops at a speed of 4 miles per hour. How far would it travel in 15 minutes?
a) 15 miles
b) 5 miles
c) 1 mile

Answer: 1 mile

Fantastic feathers

66 **Birds of paradise are the jewels in a rainforest crown.** These animals are dressed in feathers of fine colors and are adorned with crests, ruffs and streamers. Males use their bright, bold plumage to catch the attention of females, but they also do splendid dances and displays to make sure they can't be ignored!

67 **The mating dance of the male cock-of-the-rock is one of nature's most extraordinary sights.** Groups of males, with their bright-orange heads, collect on a branch near the forest floor, and put on a performance for a watching female. They flutter their wings, bob their heads and scuttle along the branch. The female mates with the male whose show has most impressed her.

▼ Male cocks-of-the-rock never hide themselves behind dull colors. Their startling plumage catches the attention of females—and predators.

68 **Wilson's bird of paradise has bare blue skin on its head, which is so bright it can be seen at night.** Males prepare a patch of ground to use as a stage, clearing it of all leaves and twigs. Their tails contain two skinny, curly silver feathers and their backs are metallic green. Like all birds of paradise, the females are not as brightly colored as their mates.

▼ When a male Raggiana bird of paradise is resting, its fan of orange-red feathers is hidden from view, but if a female nears, it will show itself in all its glory.

69 Birds of paradise live in Australia, New Guinea and some Asian islands. When dead samples of these birds were sent to Europe hundreds of years ago, their legs had been removed. This led scientists to believe that these creatures had come straight from paradise, and could not touch the ground until death, which is how they got their name.

Kaleidoscope of color

70 Rainforests are full of shades of green, but the animals that live in them are often bold and bright in color. Strong colors help animals send signals to one another in a habitat where it is easy to be hidden from view.

Postman butterfly

Birdwing butterfly

Blue morpho butterfly

▲ The wings of many butterflies are covered in tiny scales that reflect light rays to create a range of shimmering colors.

▶ A strawberry poison–dart frog from Costa Rica has bright colors to warn of the poison it has on its skin.

71 While some animals use color to draw attention to themselves, others use it to hide. Giant stick insects, like many other bugs in the forest, are patterned in mottled shades of green, gray or brown so they blend in with their surroundings. Camouflage is one way to avoid being eaten in the jungle, but there are many other ways to stay alive.

Parasol fungi

72 The forest floor is littered with brightly colored "umbrellas." These little growths, called toadstools or mushrooms, are fungi—living things that are similar to plants but do not need sunlight. Orange, gold, red, blue and yellow are common fungi colors, which may alert grazing animals to the poisons they contain.

Cup fungi

◀ The giant stick insect can reach 18 inches (45 centimeters) in length.

▲ Chameleons can change their skin color, often to make themselves attractive to possible mates.

HIDE AND SEEK

With an adult's help, use the Internet to find out how these insects use camouflage to survive:

Mantis   Glasswing butterfly
Agrippa moth   Leaf moth
Leaf insect

73 Chameleons are masters of disguise.

These lizards are able to change the color of their skin according to heat, light and their mood. When chameleons are feeling relaxed and calm they are most likely to appear green, but they can turn yellow in a flash if they are angry.

▼ Fungi grow on old trees and rotting leaves on the forest floor.

Stinkhorn

74 Scarlet macaws, with their feathers of red, blue and green, brighten up cliff faces where they settle.

They visit cliffs to eat clay, which helps them deal with poisons found in some of the seeds they eat. A flock of macaws is an explosion of color and sound. They squawk and squabble as they feed, but fall silent if a predator nears.

▶ The rainbow colors of a scarlet macaw's plumage have led to this beautiful bird being trapped for the pet trade.

The key to survival

75 Surviving in a rainforest is a battle for most animals. Food and shelter are plentiful, but habitats are so crowded it is easy for predators to hide. As a result, many creatures have developed amazing ways to stay alive.

76 Some rainforest animals pretend to be poisonous. When explorer Henry Bates (1825–1892) examined butterflies in the Amazon he found one type of patterned butterfly that tasted foul to birds, and another type that looked very similar, which didn't. He concluded that some animals copy (mimic), the appearance of others that are poisonous to avoid being eaten.

▲ Leaflitter toads are named for their clever camouflage. They resemble the decaying leaves of their forest floor habitat.

▼ Goliath tarantulas don't build webs to catch their prey — they hunt just like bigger predators, stalking animals such as frogs.

77 Poisons are common in many rainforest creatures. However, the Goliath tarantula spider uses flying hairs, as well as poisons, to keep safe! Probably the world's largest spider, it reaches 12 inches (30 centimeters) across, with 1-inch-long (2.5-centimeter-long) fangs. If threatened, Goliath tarantula spiders shoot hairs at attackers, which cause irritation and pain.

78 Rainforest ants morph (change) from black insects into red berries.
Parasite worms living inside the ants cause their rear ends to swell and turn red. Birds mistake the ants for juicy berries and eat them. The worms' eggs are then spread through the bird's droppings. Without this clever bit of mimicry, birds would not eat the ants, which taste bitter, so the worms would not be able to reproduce.

▶ Tiny termites are responsible for building large, round nests that hang on branches throughout the rainforest.

Termite nest

79 Working together means ants and termites, which live in colonies of many millions, are giants of the jungle. Termites build huge nests in trees, while leafcutter ants join forces to collect fallen leaves and carry them to their nests. The leaves become food for fungi growing in the nest, which the ants then collect and eat.

▼ Forest floors teem with columns of leafcutter ants, carrying leaf pieces more than 20 times their own body weight.

Inside the nest is a complex tunnel network

The jungle's bounty

80 When Christopher Columbus (1451–1506) trekked through the rainforests of Central America he searched in vain for treasure. Eventually, other explorers and invaders came to realize that the rainforests of the world are home to plenty of other valuables. Sadly, it is this discovery that has led to the destruction of so much of the rainforest habitat.

▼ Machines can cut and shred sugarcane at great speed. This crop is used for food and to make ethanol, a type of fuel.

81 For many people who rely on rainforests for survival, the jungle's most precious bounty is wood. Trees provide fuel for cooking, keeping warm and heating water. People also cut down large numbers of trees to sell the wood—this is called logging.

I DON'T BELIEVE IT!

Chewing gum comes from trees! It starts off as a sticky goo that is collected from chicle trees. It is then boiled, and flavors, such as mint or fruit are added.

▲ Cocoa beans grow inside pods.

▲ Latex drips into a collecting cup.

▲ Star fruits, or carambolas, can be sweet or sour.

82

Chocolate, sugar and rubber come from rainforest plants. Cocoa pods are cut open to reveal seeds (cocoa beans) which are dried, cleaned and made into chocolate. Sugar comes from a grass called sugarcane that grows in tropical areas. Rubber is harvested from trees as a white sticky gum called latex, which is made into many useful products such as tires and hoses.

83

Scientists are discovering that rainforest plants can be used to treat diseases. The people of the rainforests have known this for thousands of years. Quinine is a chemical that comes from the bark of the cinchona tree. It has been used by Amazonian Indians to prevent malaria—a deadly disease spread by mosquitoes. It is thought many rainforest plants could be used to treat cancer in the future.

► The outer bark of a cinchona tree is peeled back to reveal yellow inner bark, which contains quinine.

84

Many delicious fruits, vegetables, nuts, spices and herbs come from rainforests, although they may be cultivated (grown) in other places. Shops around the world sell ginger, cloves, pepper, nutmeg, pineapples, bananas, starfruits and sweet potatoes, all of which originally came from rainforests.

Paradise lost

85 Mangrove forests are one of the world's fastest disappearing habitats. Half of them have been destroyed in just 50 years. The trees are cut down so the swampy ground can be used to cultivate shrimps to be sold as food. Coastal areas that have lost their mangrove forests are more likely to suffer from tsunamis, storms and flooding.

86 The red-vented cockatoo is one of the world's rarest birds. Chicks are taken from nests and sold as pets—there may now be as few as 1,000 left. The giant elephant birds of Madagascar died out centuries ago when their eggs were taken for food.

87 Gold mines, which use the poisonous metal mercury, have been established in some rainforests. Water that contains mercury can kill anything that comes into contact with it, and may have caused the disappearance of many types of frog and toad.

QUIZ

Which of these words means a type of animal has completely disappeared?
a) Existing
b) Extinct
c) Extinguished

Answer:
b

▲ This mangrove swamp in Indonesia has been devastated by shrimp farming. Mangroves protect land from water damage and are home to many animals, which, once destroyed, may take centuries to recover.

88 Humans' closest relatives are being eaten to extinction. Primates such as gorillas, chimps and bonobos are sold as meat in Africa, while monkeys and langurs are served as luxury dishes in Asia. Primates also suffer when their habitats are affected by human conflicts.

89 When the forest dies, so does a way of life. Now the future looks uncertain for millions of tribal people whose families have depended on rainforests for centuries. When they lose their forest homes, it is hard for people to retain the knowledge and skills that help them to survive.

▲ WWF international staff patrols search for evidence of poaching activities in central Africa.

▶ Wild populations of great apes such as chimpanzees are disappearing fast.

Burning issues

90 Cutting down forests is called deforestation. Many forests are lost when they are turned into plantations—large fields that are used to grow single crops, such as bananas or rubber. Scientists believe that at least 19 million precious rainforest trees are cut down every day for wood or to make way for crops.

91 Around one-sixth of the Amazon rainforest has been destroyed, yet deforestation continues around the world. New roads are being built in the South American and African rainforests, which make it easier to fell trees. As many countries with rainforests are poor, selling wood can seem a good way for people to pay for food.

▼ It only takes a few hours for modern machines to fell trees and remove vegetation so the land can be used for farming.

I DON'T BELIEVE IT!

Orangutans are close to extinction because their forests are becoming palm plantations. Palm oil is used in food and as a fuel. It is expected that orangutans will be gone from the wild in less than ten years.

▶ Aerial photos show how huge areas of rainforest are being destroyed so the land can be used for cattle and crops.

92 The Amazon rainforest is being cut down to provide land for cattle.

These animals are used for beef, which is sent to the U.S. and other developed nations for use in hamburgers and similar foods. More land is cleared for cattle than for any other single use in the Amazon. There are more than 200 million herds of cattle in the region, and that number is likely to grow.

93 Large areas of rainforest are destroyed using "slash and burn."

Trees and plants are cut down, and the remains are burned. The cleared ground is then used for growing crops, or grass for cattle. This method of deforestation ruins the soil, which quickly loses all its goodness, so the farmers have to move on to a new patch of forest.

94 Deforestation has been found to affect our atmosphere and climate.

Removing these massive ecosystems could be responsible for causing longer periods of dry weather, droughts and flooding. Once forests are gone the soil is not held together so well, causing soil erosion, which means landslides become more common and plants can no longer grow.

◀ Slash and burn is used to clear the ground. When it is done too often, or over a large area, entire habitats may be changed or destroyed forever.

Forests for the future

95 We must preserve the world's rainforests if we value the people and wildlife that live in them. Less than eight percent of these ecosystems are currently strictly protected from deforestation, but governments could turn rainforests into national parks so they cannot be used for farming or logging.

▲ Tourists pay to go on canopy walks and admire the rainforests from above. Money from tourism can be used to protect these habitats and give local people jobs.

▼ Solar panels collect the sun's energy, which can be turned into electrical energy to provide light and heat.

96 Rainforest people can be shown how to use solar power to produce energy for light and cooking. Solar power is sustainable, which means it will never run out—unlike rainforest trees. Wood fires produce dirty smoke, but solar energy, which comes from the sun, is pollution-free.

97
Technology may help save the Congo rainforest in Africa. Local people who find better ways to earn money than cutting down trees will be helped with money from a special fund. Their progress will be checked using satellite images of the forest.

98
It was once thought that when a rainforest had gone, it would be gone forever. However, scientists have grown a fresh forest in Borneo to replace one that has been destroyed. Seeds from more than 1,300 trees were planted, and the soil was treated with a special fertilizer. Now 30 types of mammal and 116 types of bird have moved in. Local people have been involved with the project, and helped it to succeed.

▶ Workers at an orangutan orphanage in Borneo care for baby orangs that have lost their parents to hunting or the illegal pet trade.

99
Everyone can make a difference to the future of the rainforests. Shoppers can check they are not buying products that come from rainforest regions, and governments can develop tourism so that local people can earn a living protecting forests, rather than destroying them.

Products that may come from rainforest regions:

* Wood
* Soya
* Beef
* Palm oil

Check labels before buying

100
Rainforests will only be preserved if people respect all of Earth's delicate ecosystems. Everyone who cares about nature hopes that there is still time to halt the damage, and that rainforests will still be around in the centuries to come.

Index

Entries in **bold** refer to main subject entries. Entries in *italics* refer to illustrations.